ANIMALS IN THE CITY

Owls

Ava Podmorow

Explore other books at:
WWW.ENGAGEBOOKS.COM

VANCOUVER, B.C.

WWW.ENGAGEBOOKS.COM

Owls: Level Pre-1
Animals in the City
Podmorow, Ava 2004 –
Text © 2022 Engage Books
Design © 2022 Engage Books

Edited by: A.R. Roumanis
and Sarah Harvey

Text set in Epilogue

FIRST EDITION / FIRST PRINTING

LIBRARY AND ARCHIVES CANADA CATALOGUING IN PUBLICATION

Title: Owls / Ava Podmorow.
Names: Podmorow, Ava, author.
Description: Series statement: Animals in the city
Engaging readers: level pre-1, beginner.

Identifiers: Canadiana (print) 20220396426 | Canadiana (ebook) 20220396434
ISBN 978-1-77476-764-1 (hardcover)
ISBN 978-1-77476-765-8 (softcover)
ISBN 978-1-77476-766-5 (epub)
ISBN 978-1-77476-767-2 (pdf)

Subjects:
LCSH: Readers (Elementary)
LCSH: Readers—Owls.
LCGFT: Readers (Publications)

Classification: LCC PE1119.2 .P638 2022 | DDC J428.6/2—DC23

This project has been made possible in part
by the Government of Canada.

Canada

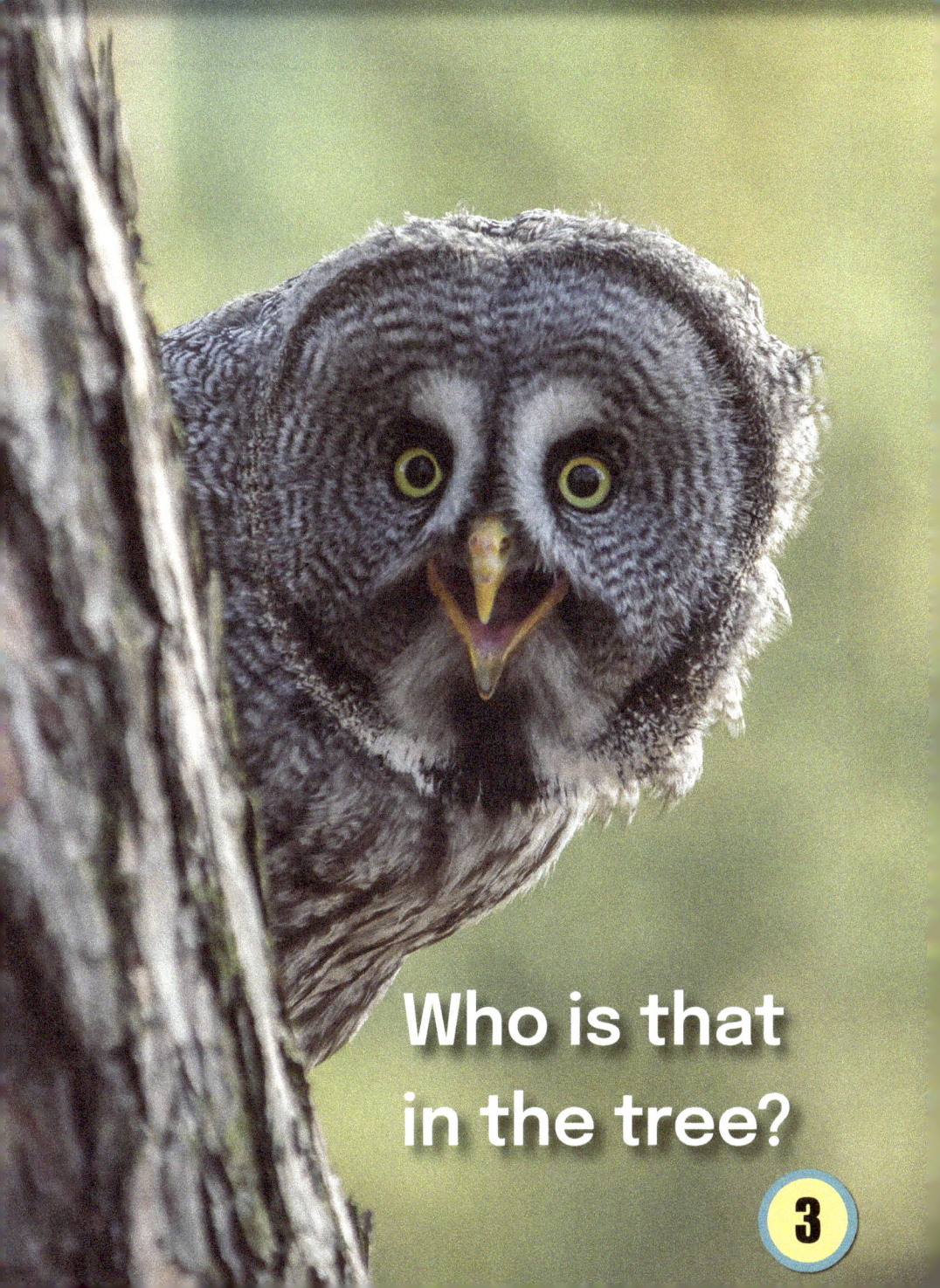

Who is that
in the tree?

Owls live in trees,
holes in the ground,
and even barns.

Wing

Owls have long feathers on their wings.

They have yellow
or orange eyes.

Eyes

Their claws
are sharp.

Claws

It is easy for owls
to find food in cities.

Owls eat
mice, bats,
and insects.

Owls like to live alone or in pairs.

13

The largest owl is the Great Horned Owl.

The smallest owl is the Elf Owl.

Owls live between 4 and 12 years in the wild.

Most owls lay
from two to five
eggs at a time.

Some kinds of owls can lay up to 13 eggs.

Most owls
sleep during
the day.

They usually
hunt at night.

Owls have eye tubes,
not eyeballs.

They can only look straight ahead.

Owls can move their heads in almost a full circle.

They can see a lot that way.

25

Owls are quiet
when they fly.

Look up here!
Hoot, hoot!

29

Explore other books in the Animals In The City series.

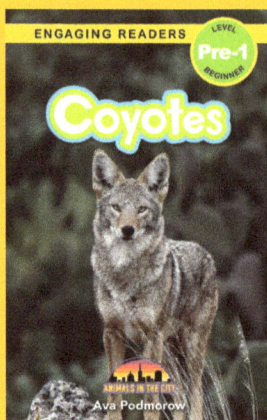

Visit www.engagebooks.com/readers

Explore level 1 readers with the Animals That Make a Difference series.

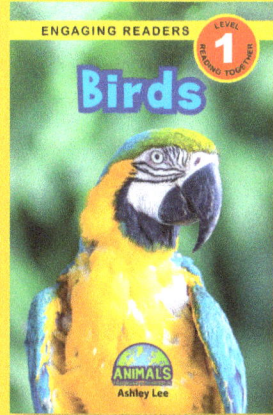

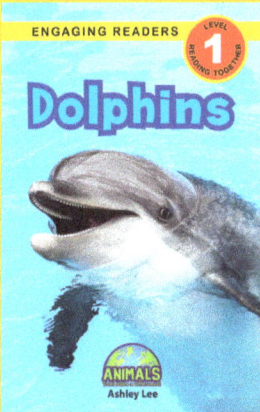

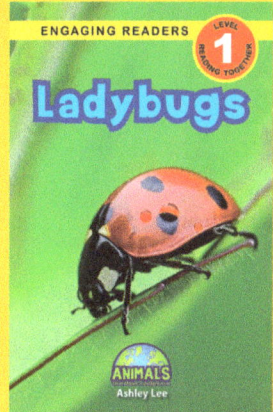

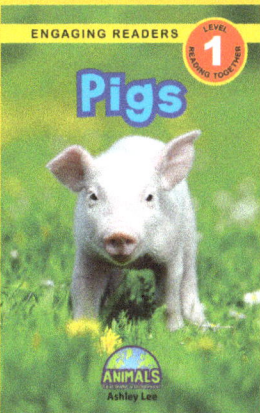

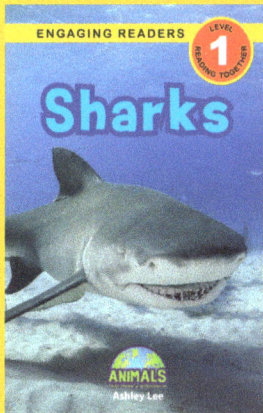

ENGAGING READERS — LEVEL 1 — READING TOGETHER

Bees
ANIMALS That Make a Difference
Jared Siemens

Bats
ANIMALS That Make a Difference
Ashley Lee

Birds
ANIMALS That Make a Difference
Ashley Lee

Dolphins
ANIMALS That Make a Difference
Ashley Lee

Horses
ANIMALS That Make a Difference
Ashley Lee

Ladybugs
ANIMALS That Make a Difference
Ashley Lee

Pigs
ANIMALS That Make a Difference
Ashley Lee

Sharks
ANIMALS That Make a Difference
Ashley Lee

Squirrels
ANIMALS That Make a Difference
Ashley Lee

Visit www.engagebooks.com/readers

www.ingramcontent.com/pod-product-compliance
Lightning Source LLC
Chambersburg PA
CBHW051239020426
42331CB00016B/3440